Creepy Crawlies

The Life Cycle of
Cockroaches

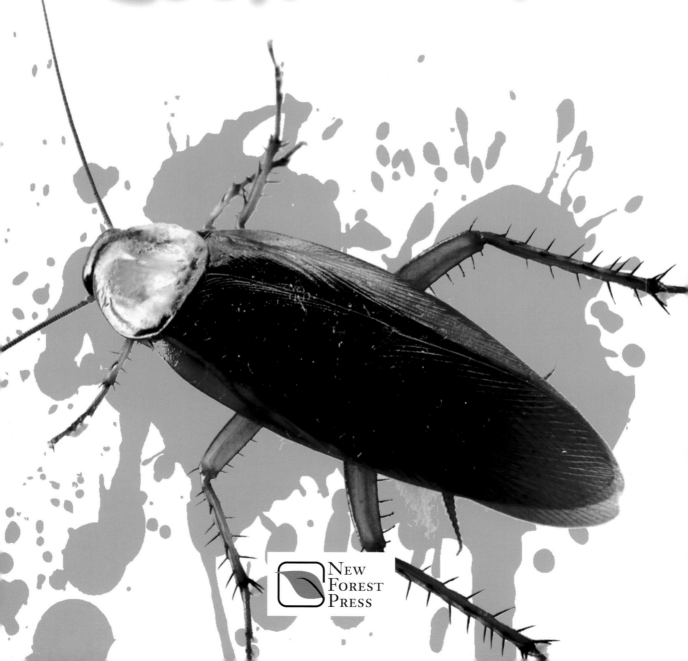

New
Forest
Press

An Hachette Company

First published in the United States by
New Forest Press, an imprint of Octopus Publishing Group Ltd

www.octopusbook.usa.com

Copyright © Octopus Publishing Group Ltd 2012

Published by arrangement with Black Rabbit Books
PO Box 784, Mankato, MN 56002

Library of Congress Cataloging-in-Publication Data

Twist, Clint.
The Life Cycle of Cockroaches / by Clint Twist.
p. cm.--- (Creepy Crawlies)
Includes index.
Summary: "Describes the life of a cockroach by explaining its body parts, habitat, and behaviors.
Explains how the cockroaches scavenge for decomposing organic material and compares the many
types of cockroaches. Includes life-cycle diagram and close-up photos of body parts"--Provided by
publisher.
ISBN 978-1-84898-518-6 (hardcover, library bound)
1. Cockroaches--Life cycles--Juvenile literature. I. Title.
QL505.5.T857 2013
595.7'28--dc23
2012003595

Printed and bound in the USA

16 15 14 13 12 1 2 3 4 5

Publisher: Tim Cook   Editor: Margaret Parrish   Designer: Steve West

Picture credits:
b=bottom; c=center; t=top; r=right; l=left
Alamy: 5b (Paul Heartfield), 17 (James Caldwell), 20-21 (Bruce Coleman Inc.). Ardea: 4 (Alan Weaving),
8b (Pat Morris). FLPA: 1, 15 side panel, 21 side panel, 23 side panel (Nigel Cattlin), 5t (Mark Moffett/
Minden Pictures), 7 side panel (Albert Mans/Foto Natura), 9, 13b, 19t (B. Borrell Casals). Getty Images:
11 side panel (Burke/Triolo Productions). Nature Picture Library: 8 main (Nick Garbutt), 15 (Pete
Oxford). The Natural History Museum, London: 23 middle. OSF: 2-3, 22 (Colin Milkins), 12 (Phototake
Inc), 13t. Premaphotos Wildlife: 14l, 14-15, 19 side panel, 26, 27b (Ken Preston-Mafham). Science
Photo Library: 11t (Barbera Strnadova), 16 (Volker Steger), 19b (Dr Morely Read), 21t (Jeff Lepore), 23t
(Martin Dohrn), 27t (George Bernard).

Every effort has been made to trace the copyright holders, and we apologize in advance for any
unintentional omissions. We would be pleased to insert the appropriate acknowledgments in any
subsequent edition of this publication.

Contents

What are Cockroaches?

Cockroaches are winged insects that like warm, damp, dirty places. They are very tough and can run quickly.

Cockroaches live alone or in small family groups consisting of a female and her young. They normally come out at night.

A mountain cockroach with nymphs about 2 hours old

A Madagascan hissing cockroach

Most cockroaches live in tropical and subtropical forests. Some cockroaches, however, have invaded human settlements. They are now found in cities around the world.

Who's Who?

Insects belong to a group of animal known as arthropods. Adult arthropods have jointed legs but no inner skeleton. Instead, they have a tough outer exoskeleton. All insects have six legs when they are adults, and most adult insects have wings and use either one pair or two pairs for flight.

Feeding on rotting fruit

In the forest

Up Close and Personal

The average cockroach is ¾–1½ in (2–4 cm) long and reddish-brown. Its tough outer covering gives it a smooth, shiny appearance.

Close-up of a dusky cockroach

The body under the covering has three parts—head, thorax, and abdomen.

The head contains antennae, eyes, a mouth, and part of the brain. The rest of the brain is along the underside of the body. Unlike most insects, a cockroach's mouth points backward.

The head is under a protective shield called a pronotum.

The thorax is the middle part of the body, where the legs and wings are attached.

The abdomen is the largest part of the cockroach's body. It contains the digestive system.

Six Legs

Insects are sometimes called hexapods because they have six legs ("hex" means six in Latin). All insects are hexapods, but not all hexapods are insects. Springtails, for instance, have six legs but are not true insects.

Don't let the leg count fool you. This springtail isn't an insect.

Unfussy Eaters

Cockroaches are not carnivores (meat-eaters) or herbivores (plant-eaters). They are omnivores, which means that they eat any plant or animal food—but only if it is dead.

American cockroaches eat animal droppings.

Cockroaches are not predators; they are scavengers. They like rotting food. Rotting, or decomposition, is when microbes (known as decomposers) break down dead animals and plants.

An Oriental cockroach eats an insect

Log Life

Wood roaches feed on fallen trees. Wood, even rotten wood, has very little nutritional value. Wood roaches can live on this poor diet thanks to a special microbe in their digestive systems. They spend their whole lives safely inside a rotten log munching away.

A wood roach spends its life eating rotting wood.

Cockroaches are part of nature's clean-up crew. They help get rid of rotting animals and plants. They also feed happily on animal droppings.

Getting Around

During the day, cockroaches hide from predators. Their flat bodies allow them to squeeze into the smallest hiding places.

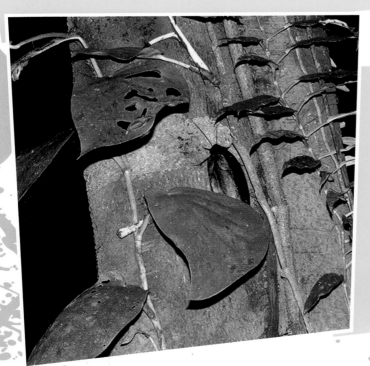

Cockroaches come out to feed at night. There are few predators around, but the roaches still move quickly. When it comes to running, cockroaches are about the fastest animals on six legs.

Cockroaches walk like other insects—they lift the middle leg on one side at the same time as the front and back legs on the other side. Three legs are always touching the ground, which makes them very stable.

Cockroaches always use the same pattern of steps.

To go from a walk to a run, insects just move their legs faster. They do not change their pattern of steps the way horses change from a walk to a canter.

Horses use different steps, depending on the speed they go.

Sprinters

When cockroaches run, they really run! They lean back and lift the front of their bodies into the air and sprint on their back legs. At full speed, they can cover 50 body lengths per second—about 10 times faster than a human runner.

Cockroaches are very fast sprinters and run on their back legs.

Finding Food

Cockroaches have poor eyesight and can only see the difference between light and dark. They make up for this by having long antennae with many sensitive receptors.

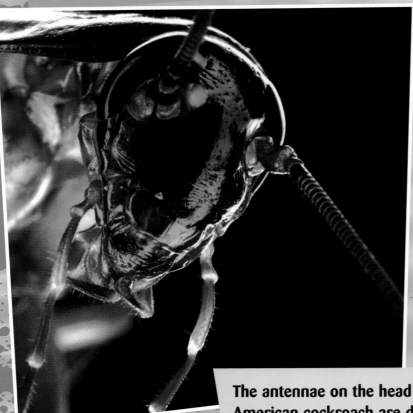

Each segment of the antennae carries sensitive receptors that the cockroach uses to find out about its surroundings.

The antennae on the head of this American cockroach are divided into about 100 segments.

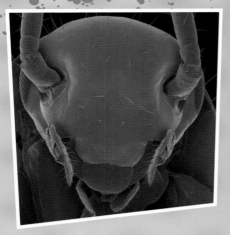

The antennae act as ears, nose, and feelers.

Some receptors sense vibrations of movement and sound. Others are sensitive to temperature; there are separate receptors for hot and cold.

The most important receptors detect smells, especially the distinctive smells made by rotting plant and animal matter.

This Oriental cockroach is cleaning its antennae.

Sensitive Legs

Cockroaches also detect vibrations through tiny bristles on their legs. While their antennae are busy finding food, their legs are alert to any movements around them.

Supersensitive hairs

Bad Habits

Cockroaches are smelly. Rotting meat and plants smell nasty, but cockroaches can smell even worse.

Camouflage is another form of self-defense. This cockroach looks like a dead leaf.

Smell can be used for self-defense. If threatened by a predator, a roach squirts a cloud of foul-smelling liquid. When the predator retreats, the cockroach runs away.

This cockroach's self-defense system failed—it's being eaten by a scorpion!

The smell a cockroach makes might be a message to other roaches saying, "Here is plenty of food." Or it might mean the opposite: "Keep away, this food is mine."

Dirty Bugs

Cockroaches are very unclean. They leave a trail of droppings wherever they go. Because their mouths point backward, they have to walk all over their food to eat it. They even leave droppings on food they have yet to eat.

A German cockroach walking over food and leaving droppings

Australian cockroaches eating cake

Infrequent Flyers

Both male and female roaches have wings, but the females of most species cannot fly. Only males can fly, but they rarely do.

Male and female cockroaches usually live completely separate lives. At mating time, the females release special smells known as pheromones.

This German cockroach will use his antennae to detect a female.

Certain smell receptors on the male's antennae can detect the faintest trace of female pheromones in the air. He will follow this scent to the waiting female. If the male cannot find the female, he lands and releases his own pheromones. These are not as strong as the female's, but they help her find him in the darkness.

Two American cockroaches mating

The male American cockroach only uses his wings to find a mate.

Girls Only

Not all creatures mate to produce young. Some insect species, such as the Surinam roach, are all female. They produce fertile eggs on their own. This process is known as parthenogenesis.

The Surinam roach does not need a male to reproduce.

Egg Cases

There are over 4,000 species of cockroach. After mating, most females lay their eggs inside a special egg case called an ootheca. It can contain six to 50 eggs.

Some species of cockroach carry the ootheca around for several days before leaving it in a dark, damp place. Others carry it for several weeks, until the eggs hatch.

A smoky brown cockroach's ootheca

All oothecae have a smooth, leathery outer surface. A raised seam called a keel runs along one edge. Tiny openings at the base allow the eggs inside to breathe.

An Oriental cockroach with its ootheca

A few types of cockroach do not lay their eggs at all. Instead, the eggs develop inside the female's abdomen. The young cockroaches, called nymphs, are born live.

A female cockroach after giving birth to her live young

Development

Insects develop from eggs in two different ways. With some, including cockroaches and grasshoppers, the eggs hatch into nymphs that look like the adults. With other kinds of insect, such as bees and beetles, the eggs hatch into larvae that look very different from the adults. The larvae go through metamorphosis, which is when they change into adults.

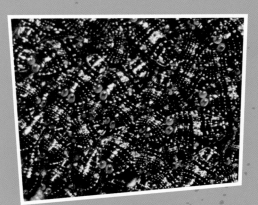

Brightly colored nymphs

Nymph's Progress

Young cockroaches look like miniature adults, but they are incomplete. It can take 10 months for nymphs to reach adulthood. During this time, they shed their "skin" many times.

This cockroach has just shed its exoskeleton.

Insects have an exoskeleton that protects their bodies, but it does not stretch. As an insect grows, it forms a new exoskeleton before shedding the old one.

An eastern milk snake shedding its skin

Growth Stages

With each instar, the nymphs become more complete. For example, newly hatched nymphs have no wings, and their antennae have about 25 segments, compared with the 100 or so segments adults have. Until the nymph reaches its final molt, its wings and antennae will not be fully functional.

The process by which an animal sheds its outer covering is called molting. This term is used with insects, other arthropods, and snakes.

Newly hatched nymphs are almost colorless, but they soon turn darker. They molt up to 12 times before they are adults. The stages between each molt are called instars.

Adult and nymph American cockroaches

Cockroaches and Humans

Cockroaches are most at home in warm, wet woodlands, but they find human settlements inviting, too.

Houses that are comfortable for people are also comfortable for cockroaches. They provide everything roaches need—heat, dampness, and lots of organic waste.

Invading a kitchen

About 20 cockroach species are so closely attached to human settlements that they have become serious pests. Among the worst are the German cockroach (which actually comes from Africa), the Oriental cockroach, and the American cockroach. They are found in cities around the world and live under floors and between walls, especially in bathrooms and kitchens.

German cockroach

Oriental cockroach

American cockroach

Spoilage

Cockroaches not only eat food, but also spoil it. Because they scatter their droppings everywhere, cockroaches spoil about a thousand times more food than they consume.

An Oriental cockroach spoiling a piece of bread

Unusual Behavior

Some cockroaches do unusual things—well, unusual for cockroaches. Not only do the largest species grow to an amazing 3 in (7.5 cm), but the fastest roaches are entered in races by their human owners.

Hissing monster

The Madagascan giant cockroach is big—3 in (7.5 cm)—and noisy.

It uses sound as a defense. When disturbed, it puffs up its body with air and huffs out the air through openings in its body, making a loud hissing sound that scares off predators.

Parental care

Wood roaches are unusual in that they care for their young—most roaches don't. When the nymphs hatch, they lack the microbes needed to feed on wood. They eat their mother's droppings until they absorb enough microbes from the droppings to be able to digest wood on their own.

Speed demon

No roach is faster than the American cockroach. This amazing insect can cover a distance of 5 ft (1.5 m) a second—that's five times faster than a German cockroach.

At the races

In some places, cockroach racing is a sport. Races are run around a circular track. Roaches that do not start running right away may be prodded into action.

Sizes and Shapes

Although cockroaches have the same basic body parts, they vary considerably in shape, size, and color.

Leaf cockroach
This West African cockroach hides from daytime predators by standing still on the forest floor. It is perfectly camouflaged as a fallen yellow leaf.

Tropical giant

Native to the tropical forests of Central America, this is one of the largest cockroaches in the world. It can measure over 3 in (7.5 cm).

Banana roach

The green banana roach does not invade homes. Still, it is a pest because it eats crops.

Live birth

The Cape Mountain cockroach lives in highland forest in southern Africa. Unlike most cockroaches, it does not lay its eggs in an ootheca. The eggs remain inside the female until the nymphs hatch.

Find Out More

Life Cycle

Most female cockroaches lay their eggs in a special case called an ootheca. The eggs hatch into nymph instars, which molt about 12 times before becoming adults.

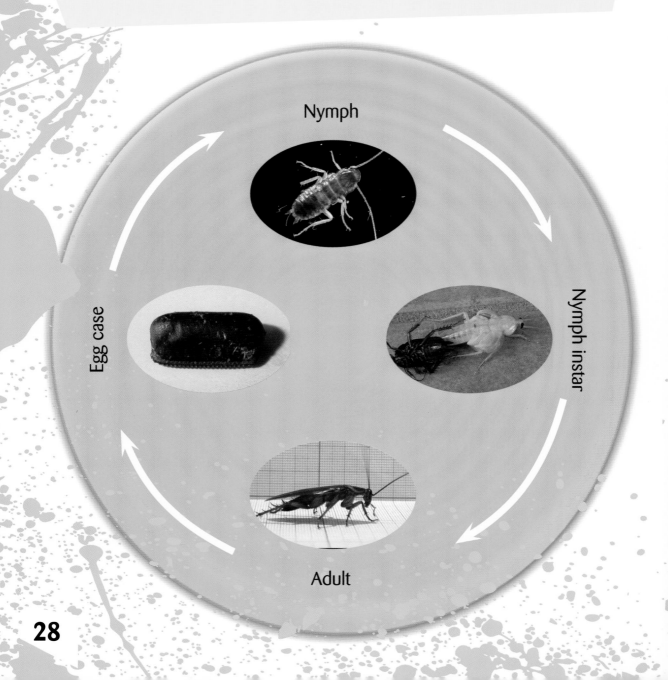

Nymph

Nymph instar

Egg case

Adult

Fabulous Facts

Fact 1: Cockroaches breathe through holes in their sides called spiracles.

Fact 2: Cockroaches cannot see in red light, but they can see very well in green light.

Fact 3: Cockroaches get their sense of smell from their antennae.

Fact 4: A cockroach's mouth contains the senses of smell and taste. It moves from side to side, not up and down, the way human mouths do.

Fact 5: Cockroaches live up to two years.

Fact 6: Some humans are allergic to cockroaches.

Fact 7: The brain of a cockroach is scattered along the underside of its belly. That's why if a cockroach's head is cut off, it can survive for up to a week. It finally dies of thirst.

Fact 8: Cockroaches have been present on Earth for more than 400 million years.

Fact 9: There are approximately 4,000 types of cockroach.

Fact 10: Most cockroaches have 18 knees.

Fact 11: Some kinds of cockroach can hold their breath for 40 minutes.

Fact 12: Cockroaches thrive in nearly every corner of the globe, despite our best efforts to get rid of them.

Fact 13: Cockroaches' eyes are made up of 4,000 lenses, which is why they can see in all directions at the same time.

Glossary

Abdomen—the largest part of an insect's three-part body; the abdomen contains many important organs.

Antennae—a pair of special sense organs found at the front of the head on most insects.

Arthropod—any creepy crawly that has jointed legs; insects and spiders are arthropods.

Bristles—short, strong hairs.

Decomposers—microscopic plants and animals that break down the dead bodies of other plants and animals.

Exoskeleton—a hard outer covering that protects and supports the bodies of insects.

Functional—in working order.

Insect—a kind of creepy crawly that has six legs; most insects also have wings.

Instar—a stage between molts for a developing insect nymph.

Larva—a wormlike creature that is the juvenile (young) stage in the life cycle of many insects.

Microbes—tiny living things so small that they can only been seen through a powerful microscope.

Molting—the process of shedding the body's surface layer so that it can be replaced by a fresh one.

Nymph—the juvenile (young) stage in the life cycle of insects that do not produce larvae.

Omnivore—an animal that eats both plants and meat.

Ootheca—egg case produced by female cockroaches.

Parasite—any living thing that lives or feeds on or in the body of another living thing.

Parthenogenesis—the production of young by females without the involvement of males. Some insect species consist entirely of females.

Pheromone—a scent substance produced by many kinds of animal that is used to communicate certain information or "messages."

Predator—an animal that hunts and eats other animals.

Pronotum—a tough shield that protects the head of some cockroaches.

Pupation—the process by which insect larvae change their body shape to the adult form.

Receptors—tiny organs that detect things such as smell, heat, and vibration.

Rotting—the process of decomposition by which the bodies of dead animals and plants are broken down.

Scavenger—an animal that eats dead and rotting plants and animals.

Segment—a part of something that is divided into a number of similar parts.

Skeleton—an internal structure of bones that supports the bodies of large animals such as mammals, reptiles, and fish.

Springtail—a six-legged creepy crawly that is not a true insect.

Sprinting—running on two legs at top speed.

Subtropical—belonging to a region near the Earth's equator where the climate is always warm.

Thorax—the middle part of an insect's body where the legs are attached.

Tropical—belonging to the region around the Earth's equator where the climate is always hot.

Index